Amir Fathizadeh

GOSSIP
The Road to Ruin

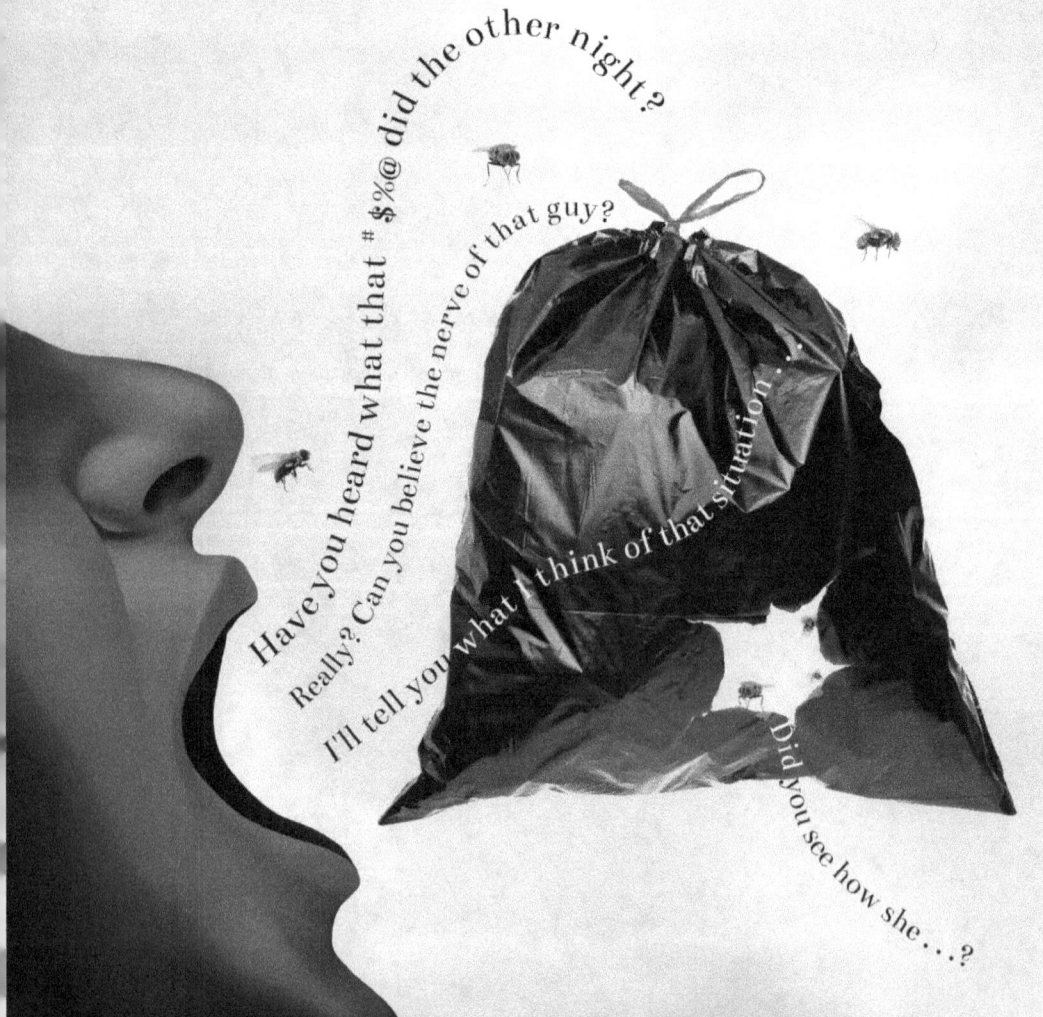

GOSSIP
Copyright © 2019, 2020 by Amir Fathizadeh

All rights reserved. No part of this publication may be reproduced, distributed, or transmitted in any form or by any means, including photocopying, recording, or other electronic or mechanical methods, without the prior written permission of the author, except in the case of brief quotations embodied in critical reviews and certain other non-commercial uses permitted by copyright law.

Tellwell Talent
www.tellwell.ca

ISBN
978-0-2288-2438-1 (Hardcover)
978-0-2288-2437-4 (Paperback)
978-0-2288-2439-8 (eBook)

Praise for Gossip, The Road to Ruin

"This engaging, easy to read book presents us all with a critical challenge in our daily life: how can we be more authentic and act compassionately and with love? Were all of us to heed its message, we could move our society to a higher level of connection and grace. Amir, as always, has a clear eye to what will benefit us all, and conveys it in a humorous and highly readable way. His guidance and coaching has changed my life, and that of my family, for which we are forever thankful."

Robin Quon, Attorney At Law

"We all know how it feels to be the subject of gossip. We know the pain it causes in families, schools, and workplaces. We understand how counterproductive and detrimental it is, but when have we ever take the time to dissect the reasons we gossip, the problems it causes, and then actively work to eliminate it? Amir Fathizadeh has done this for us! Packed with stories, analogies, and practical exercises, this book will help you become a stronger communicator while preserving relationships and fostering a positive environment around you."

Jon Denney, President, Professional Business Coaches Alliance Syracuse, New York

"I have known Amir for over 5 years. We are professional business coaching peers and a good friends. I know him to be a passionate, committed and motivated life and business coach. Kudos to Amir for tackling a subject that few have dared to address. The topic of Gossip indeed deserved the attention that Amir's new book has provided. It is an interesting and informative read. Gossip will be enjoyed by all and will provide an excellent complement to anyone seeking guidance from a life and/or business coaching perspective, as it will deliver insights that are helpful in addressing leadership behavior improvement opportunities as well as becoming a more effective communicator by improving listening skills. I enjoyed reading Gossip and know that you will too!"

Elio Cozzi
Achieve Business Coaching and Consulting

"Gossip is one of the most insightful personal growth books I've read in recent years. Definitely gave me lots of food for thought. Not being prone to gossip myself, I had never given it much thought. But, reading Amir's book shed a whole new light on the subject and it was a real eye-opener. Thinking back about many of my past experiences, both personally and in business, I realized I had probably missed some important clues about what was going on with some people around me. In retrospect, I was probably too dismissive of some people's problems because I didn't realize what was going on behind the scenes. Since reading Gossip, I'm now more on the lookout for the hidden agendas of certain people."

Dick Kuiper, Founder, Spinnaker Marketing

"Wow, a great book…and very enlightening. I've always avoided gossipers because I was never sure how to handle them without starting an argument. In his book entitled Gossip, Mr. Fathizadeh provided a detailed explanation of how gossip starts and gets out of control.

The book gave me all the ammunition I need to call a person's bluff when I suspect gossip is at the root of a problem. I no longer have to shy away from heated discussions torched from a piece of gossip, but confront the guilty party before things get out of control."

Troy Hesselgesser, Construction Manager - Retired

GOSSIP
The Road to Ruin

How We Make Enemies and Alienate People

First Edition – 2019

ACKNOWLEDGMENTS

First and foremost, I'd like to thank some amazing people in my life. Special thanks to my granddaughter, Meela, who encourages me to live my life day by day, full of excitement and energy. This book is dedicated to my grandchildren Alden, Dori, Theron, Meela and Charlotte in hope that someday they will choose to have lives without negative gossip and that they will be responsible for creating a peaceful environment where everyone can communicate properly. I hope this book will be a reference for them to create that kind of environment. It is with the commitment and proper education that this generation can someday eliminate destructive gossip from our society.

I would also like to acknowledge my wife, Sandra, who at first questioned me writing a book and then became a big fan of the book and helped design the cover. Her opinion and her ideas most often make the biggest difference.

I acknowledge and am grateful for my three grown children, Azar, Bijan and Arash, who have dealt with many issues in their own lives. My commitment is that they'll be able to take what is in this book and make a difference in their work environments, with their friends and in all of their relationships.

I wish to also extend my heartfelt thanks to my friend, Robin Quon, who was an inspiration during the process. She helped edit several drafts. I am grateful for her friendship and support.

MEET THE AUTHOR

Amir Fathizadeh is an international speaker and program leader who conducts life-changing programs in North America for thousands of people. A life coach and certified business coach, also well-versed in emotional intelligence, he's been delivering programs in Leadership, Relationships, Emotional Intelligence, Communication, Behaviors and how are views get in the way to ordinary individuals, business owners, managers and CEOs for twenty years.

Amir is an expert in Behavioral Analysis. In this training he explains to his audiences and clients why they have certain behavior styles, how other people perceive them, how they can identify other people's styles, and how to interact with each style.

His unique approach and methodology guide his audience to discover their blind spots and take their personal and professional lives to new levels of success.

TABLE OF CONTENTS

Chapter 1	Introduction	1
Chapter 2	The Evolution of Gossip	5
Chapter 3	Like Charity, Gossip Begins at Home	9
Chapter 4	Unlike Charity, Gossip Has an Ugly Downside	21
Chapter 5	Why We Persist	29
Chapter 6	Listen More; You'll Gossip Less	39
Chapter 7	Technology: Gossip's New Frontier	51
Chapter 8	Gossip's Impact	57
Chapter 9	Motivation to Stop Gossiping	69
Chapter 10	Ending the Vicious Cycle	75
Chapter 11	Gossip in the Workplace	79
Chapter 12	Combating Workplace Gossip	87
Appendix A - The Evolution of Gossip: The Rest of the Story		95

Chapter 1
INTRODUCTION

"It is easier to dam a river than to stop gossip."
—Filipino proverb

For many people, the subject of gossip does not seem like a very controversial one. It is what it is – right?

Not really. I see it to be a complex and multi-faceted topic. Throughout the course of my personal life and business career, I've found that gossip has been a profound and impactful factor in my own life and that of friends and associates around me.

During my more than forty years as a college student, a corporate employee, a small business owner and a youth soccer coach, I found gossip to have a huge cadre of negative effects. I became a transformational course leader in the US and Canada and began to formulate a deeper understanding of the impact of gossip.

After becoming a Life Coach and Certified Professional Business Coach, it became clear this aspect of life

INTRODUCTION

needed to be addressed in-depth in order to make our workplaces and homes more peaceful and productive. My expertise in Emotional Intelligence gave me a unique perspective on this issue.

After presenting countless seminars on the topic of gossip, and seeing the difference it made for my audiences, I decided the time had come ... the time to write a book presenting a comprehensive picture of the complexities of gossip and the harm it can and does cause.

I have gathered together all the tools and wisdom I have gained about this topic over several decades and share them with you in this book. My hope is that the expression of my views and accumulated expertise in this area will aid the process of healing of individuals, families, business environments and society in general.

Probably the best place to start is to look at the definition of the word gossip itself.

> *Gossip [gos-uhp] – noun*
> 1. idle talk or rumor, especially about the personal or private affairs of others
> 2. light, familiar talk or writing

Here we have two different versions of the definition. To many readers, these may seem similar. In real life, however, I've found them to be drastically different regarding the effect they have on the people involved.

Definition #2 is what I refer to as the "entertainment"

version of gossip. It is what we might see in various gossip columns, in print or other media, and largely involve celebrities or other well-known people. While they can often come across as nasty, the primary thrust is to gain readership.

This same part of the definition covers what I call conversational small talk – not really intended to harm anyone but simply casual chit-chat in the spirit of human discourse.

Definition #1, however, is where we find the often mean-spirited barbs on the negative side of gossip, usually aimed at inflicting harm on others. This is the definition I'll be concentrating on in this book. It is very important for you, as the reader, to thoroughly understand the significant difference between the two.

From this point on, I'll be referring to this mean-spirited buzz as malicious gossip. When you utter gossip yourself or hear it from others, you'll usually be able to tell very quickly whether it's truly malicious gossip or simply its harmless counterpart.

Three Gossip Arenas

Almost all malicious gossip takes place on one of three playing fields: family, social groups or the workplace. I'll be addressing each of these groups individually, but keep in mind there are many commonalities that transcend the three groups.

In general, from a cause-and-effect perspective, the family and workplace groups are at opposite ends of

INTRODUCTION

the spectrum, while social groups are in the middle, representing a blending of the other two groups.

Chapter 2
THE EVOLUTION OF GOSSIP

A cruel story runs on wheels, and every hand oils the wheels as they turn.
—Ouida, aka Maria Louise Ramé

Nobody seems to know the real story of how gossip started in the human race.

The term has been researched with respect to its origins in evolutionary psychology and found to be an important means for people to monitor cooperative reputations within a society.

It therefore provides a conduit to support indirect reciprocity among groups and individuals. This indirect reciprocity is a social interaction where one person helps another with an exchange of information and is then assisted by a third person ... and so on.

This theory was originated by Robin Dunbar in a research article, entitled "Gossip in Evolutionary Perspective," published in 2004. Dunbar is an evolutionary biologist whose studies indicated that gossip promotes social bonding in large groups.

Dunbar goes on to point out that conversation is a uniquely human phenomenon. His analysis indicates that about two-thirds of human conversation time is devoted to social topics, most of which can be given the generic label of gossip.

His theory involving social bonding claims that the art of gossip can be traced back to social grooming among primates.

Regarding human interaction, Dunbar presents evidence in his study that, aside from servicing social intercommunication, a key function of gossip may be related explicitly to controlling free riders. A "free rider" is a person who benefits from something without expending effort or receiving monetary compensation. In other words, free riders are those who reap benefits without contributing their fair share.

In the sixteenth century, the word "gossip" referred to a person, most often a woman, who delighted in idle talk.

I realize that statement may seem offensive at first glance, so I'll put it in its proper perspective.

It does not mean women are more talkative than men. So, it follows that women are better conversationalists than men. They are also more adept at expressing their feelings. It just so happens that gossip sessions often make ideal forums for expressing one's feelings. Sorry guys, that's simply not our forte.

Unfortunately, society frequently associates gossipers with "newsmongers" or "tattlers." That's a downside of idle gossip, whether ill-intended or not.

In the nineteenth century, the term's definition was extended. "Gossip," as a noun, went from being used to describe the talker to the conversation between two such persons.

The verb "to gossip," meaning "to be a gossip," first appeared, like so many things in our culture, in the writings of William Shakespeare. In *Comedy of Errors*, he used it as a verb when he wrote: "With all my heart, I'll gossip at this feast."

So, enough for now on how the art of gossip got started. While there is still more to be said on the beginnings and historical evolution of gossip, let's put the rest of it aside for now and get back to the main thrust of my primary subject: examining the damage that is usually done by malicious gossip and how we can all work at alleviating it … or hopefully eliminating it altogether.

Refer to Appendix A for supplemental information on how gossiping got started and how it has evolved over time.

Chapter 3
LIKE CHARITY, GOSSIP BEGINS AT HOME

Gossip needn't be false to be evil – there's a lot of truth that shouldn't be passed around.
—Frank A. Clark

Regardless of where you are from, what language you speak or what color of skin you have, human beings all engage in gossip.

Throughout my life, I have watched many friends' families fall apart due to harmful gossip. Personally, I have also witnessed the detrimental impact of gossip in my professional life and in my own family over the years.

In adulthood, I have seen social groups, employee teams and even major companies endure huge amounts of stress dealing with a toxic culture spawned by malicious gossip.

When reading self-help books or stories involving lessons learned, it always helps to understand the author's background. The context of a writer's observations can only be accurately perceived if the reader knows details of the writer's background.

Wealthy people have an entirely different frame of reference from those of meager means. People coming from broken homes have a different perspective from those coming from stable family environments. Such differences may slant the assessment of the subject matter in one direction or another.

That being the case, I will fill you in on a little of my background:

When I look back on my life, I recognize that I was born and raised in a society filled with people who gossip. Of course, I did not realize it then, but now, I see that quite clearly.

I was born in the 1950s. My family was a very loving, middle-class family. My father was a moderately successful businessman. It was his sole priority in life to provide a good living for our family. He wanted every one of us to have as many opportunities as possible to have rewarding lives.

My mother was a wonderful woman. She did not participate in gainful employment outside our home. As a housewife, my mother's main priority was our family. She toiled all day long making sure our home was neat, clean and well-organized. Mom always made sure we got to school on time and did our homework.

At the end of the day, after all that was done, she wanted

to feel certain that we were all well-fed and as satisfied with our home environment as possible. I never took that for granted. She was amazing.

As I grew up, I felt fortunate that we lived close to many members of my extended family. I had several aunts and uncles living in close proximity, so I had quite a few cousins, nieces and nephews in my life on a daily basis.

I look back on those early days fondly, especially when I realize that almost no one's childhood is ideal and many children grow up amidst uncertainty, chaos and strife. When I reflect on it, it seemed like everyone in my family circle was always together.

Proximity and Familiarity Can Breed Gossip

Still, I grew up in a culture where gossip was simply a way of life. Chatty talk over the hedge and on the street corner was a regular form of cheap entertainment for many people, friends and family included.

As a teenage boy, I closely watched how members of my family behaved around each other. One moment they would pretend to be kind to someone present in the group. In many cases, however, once that person was gone, they would switch faces and begin talking negatively behind their back.

It wasn't just speculation on my part. Their talk was often merciless.

A Dose of Reality

Let me give you an example of my family's gossiping:

My mother had a rocky relationship with one of her daughters-in-law. When they disagreed, they rarely talked it out. Instead, my mother would talk to her sister about the spat while my sister-in-law would vent to her own mother or her husband.

This only made the problem more serious by involving additional people in the dispute. It made the problem more difficult to resolve because others were put in the position of having to choose a side.

But wait, it gets worse.

When the mother and daughter-in-law went to their individual confidants, they would naturally explain only their side of the story. With others swept up in the conflict, fuel was added to the fire. Confusion was also added to the mix since the sideline actors had only bits and pieces of the big picture.

Gossip participants can easily become combatants, and everyone becomes upset. I've seen feuds started like this go on for years.

At that time, I was far too young to really recognize what was going on. This type of gossip was the norm in my culture. As the years went on, I was somewhat surprised to see that I had inadvertently inherited this behavioral pattern. In my mind, I realized it was a nasty habit. In spite of that internal acknowledgment, trying to break it proved a monumental task.

Gossiping was an all too common pastime for people in my community – better than anything on the radio or television. The sources of new material were virtually endless and always readily available. The motivations to create or pass on gossip varied from person to person and situation to situation. Rarely was the news positive.

On the one hand, gossip seemed quite juicy. It could be intoxicatingly pleasurable. On the other hand, gossip tended to make the unknowing targets miserable when word eventually got back to them.

Since I was still far too young to truly understand how I was contributing to this negative cycle, I continued on as though nothing was amiss. Trying to do something about the problem never occurred to me at the time.

Later in life, as I became an adult, I took the opportunity to take a really long, deep look at my behavior and at myself. Slowly, I began to unravel the deep, subtle and harmful impact gossip had on my life and on the lives of other people that I loved.

As I looked back on those times as a grown man, I saw quite a different picture of the situation than the one I saw as a youngster.

During the years I spent attaining my college degrees, and later, through many more years establishing myself as a successful business person, my views about gossip became crystal clear.

I see now that malicious gossip is actually a very destructive force for almost anyone who engages in it. Gossip, when it goes unchecked, has the capacity to break families apart, devastate healthy relationships, erode trust and even disrupt business dealings.

The Road to Understanding

To truly remedy the malicious gossip disorder, we must first clearly establish exactly what it is in all its various forms. Only then can we properly launch our journey to reach meaningful solutions.

People often talk behind each other's backs in a smug manner, intending to gain other's approval or favor. It seems gossip is, unfortunately, part of who we are. But after looking at it closely, I learned that it does not have to be. I believe the tendency to gossip is more environmental than physiological. And we can certainly overcome such environmental influences – but only if we work at it.

In this book, we will open up a dialogue about gossip. We will examine why people gossip. We will look at what motivates people to gossip. Most importantly, we will look at the impact of gossip and cover strategies and tips on how to alter that behavior.

I congratulate you on having decided to pick up this book. Obviously, you must recognize that gossip in some form has affected you, members of your family, your friends, your employees and/or your co-workers, or perhaps you have witnessed others gossip but have not been involved in it yourself, or you are just curious what this book is about.

You may just now be developing an awareness that you gossip and want to stop it but are not sure how to do so. Maybe you are like me and have been engrossed in the habit so long, it's hard to see what life looks like without gossip. After all, gossip can be quite intoxicating. Or maybe you are simply the type of person who likes to read and is always looking for methods of self-improvement.

Regardless of why you have chosen to read this book, I promise you that if you are willing to take in what I cover in this book and commit to working through the exercises I present here, you will be able to transform yourself and your environment.

The Ugly Truth

Back in chapter one, I gave you the parochial dual definition of gossip and highlighted the two basic types: the innocuous and the malicious.

Since we're concentrating on the latter, let's drill down into a deeper definition:

The Oxford Dictionary's definition of gossip is as follows: "Casual or unconstrained conversation or reports about other people, typically involving details that are not confirmed as being true."

The Cambridge Dictionary's definition sounds a little harsher: "Conversation or reports about other peoples' private lives that might be unkind, disapproving, or not true."

Here's my own spin on gossip to set the tone for the remainder of this book. Since I'm focusing this book strictly on malicious gossip, I'll drop the adjective "malicious" and refer to it purely as gossip from this point forward.

Here's the hypothetical situation. You're having a conversation with someone about another person who is not present. In that conversation you invalidate, make small, demean, or simply throw the other person under the bus for whatever reason. That is gossip, plain and simple.

On the flip side, gossip is often providing news to a friend about another person, or discussing some celebrity's actions or pontificating on the political views of politicians. That's non-malicious gossip – simple, everyday conversation – and not addressed in this book.

It is the nature of the information communicated, whether nasty, mean-spirited or otherwise negative, that brings it into the realm of malicious gossip.

How did I come to this conclusion?

What I once saw as benign chatter, I began to see as a lack of honest communication. People were talking to one another, sure, but they weren't communicating in an honest and straightforward way. They were choosing to talk and gossip amongst themselves about someone else's circumstances, problems or behaviors. Rather than talk to the subject person directly, they were talking behind his or her back.

As I was growing up, I often saw gossip manifest itself

when one family member was upset with another family member. Maybe something had happened or a few unkind words had been said. But instead of approaching the problem directly with the targeted party, the family member would gossip to a third party, typically someone else in the immediate or extended family.

In passing on the gossip, the irritated family member would seek out a gossip partner who would likely take his or her side. They would express the incident in a way that made the other person feel sorry for them.

They would do this by purposely leaving out certain details or uttering outright lies. The true heart of the matter would seldom see the light of day.

When that third party passed the gossip on to yet another person in the gossip chain, the situation worsened – usually in dramatic fashion.

Eventually, gossip becomes a cycle. It is a cycle as vicious and corrosive as any other we as humans undertake. When a person learns they have been the subject of gossip – and make no mistake, they will find out – they will become understandably upset, perhaps even unjustly betrayed.

As the string of "poor me" conversations spirals downward, the opportunity to actually work through the core problem of the two primary players disappears.

The cycle can go on and on – sometimes for years – and the wounds only continue to fester.

.... **Exercise #1 – How Stories Mutate**

Here's an exercise to demonstrate how a gossip story can get mutated as it passes along the gossip chain. This exercise should be done with four or five participants, though three often works well too.

The moderator – that's you in most cases – writes up a juicy story that makes good gossip. It must contain at least two primary characters, one or two controversial incidents, a few pieces of evidence and a few personal judgments. It can be less than 100 words in length.

Without the others overhearing, the moderator then tells that story to the first participant. Just as in real-life gossip, the recipient does not take notes. Next, the first participant whispers the story to the second participant. The second participant then whispers it to the third participant … and so on.

After the last participant has heard the story, he or she repeats it out loud to the group. Then the moderator reads the original story to the group. I believe everyone will be astounded by the drastically different versions.

In one of my first-hand experiences with one of these exercises, everyone in the group found it to be not only informative but quite entertaining. There is usually lots of laughter and light-hearted finger-pointing as the various players try to figure out who dropped the ball the most. I usually find it hilarious.

The point here is that as a conversation passes verbally from person to person it easily becomes distorted, on purpose or by accident.

……… **End of Exercise**

If you are reading this book out of interest in the title, you might be very familiar with this dilemma. It is very likely that you have already recognized the countless problems gossip can cause.

Perhaps gossip has negatively affected your home and family life. Perhaps it has infected your workplace to the point where you're uncomfortable going into the office in the morning. Maybe your once strong, healthy relationships have fallen on hard times because you have been caught up in a cycle of gossip.

This book will not only help you identify the problem of gossip in your life, but it will help you come up with practical strategies on how to combat it.

Chapter 4

UNLIKE CHARITY, GOSSIP HAS AN UGLY DOWNSIDE

It is just as cowardly to judge an absent person as it is wicked to strike a defenseless one. Only the ignorant and narrow-minded gossip, for they speak of persons instead of things.

—Lawrence G. Lovasik

Recently I became aware of a situation that was going on within a family of a known business associate. This particular family was quite large. The siblings included three sisters and five brothers. One of the sisters – I'll call her Laura – loved to gossip. It was not unusual for her to share stories with others about members of the family. In a large family, she had ample material for such banter.

Not surprisingly for a habitual gossip, most of the stories Laura told were not true.

My business associate – I'll call him Steve – happened to know this family on a personal level and was invited to one of their family gatherings. It was a nice affair and everyone in attendance seemed quite friendly.

Several days later, however, Steve became aware that Laura had taken it upon herself to make up a story about him. He was shocked by what he heard. It really didn't make sense to Steve at all.

Apparently, Laura told one of her sisters that Steve said something negative about another member of her family – we'll call her Sarah. Laura started this rumor out of the blue, and soon enough, Sarah naturally became upset. This was of course understandable. She had every right to be angry because she knew Steve very well and they had a trusting relationship.

A few days after that gathering, Sarah picked up the phone and called Steve's sister. She needed someone to talk to about what had happened and was a little timid to call Steve directly.

When Steve's sister, now the third party in the gossip chain, approached him with what she learned, Steve became even more upset. Obviously, he was surprised because he had never said what she told him she heard. More than that, Steve was adamant that he would never say anything like that.

While Steve's sister knew he would never say such things, she called just to be certain it was not a slip of the tongue. Laura's sister also knew the rumor was something completely false and that Laura had made it up.

How did the various parties know what really happened?

It's simply because they have had that kind of experience with Laura in the past. Spreading rumors like this is a way for the gossiper to become popular ... at least in his or her own mind. They don't realize that in the big picture, their spiteful gossip actually diminishes their standing within the group.

Laura desperately wanted to be liked by the family, but she was not aware of the kind of damage she was creating in her own life.

Fortunately for everyone, this scenario ended pretty quickly, mostly because Steve confronted Laura about the sham. In some cases, the offended party never confronts the perpetrator; it just gets swept under the rug. Often the offended sweeps it under the rug, but carries around an unspoken grudge or creates his or her own story about the perpetrator.

I have learned over the years that this kind of confrontation between the offended party and the gossip-monger is the best remedy. It not only brings the situation at hand to a tidy closure, but it serves to give notice to the gossiping party that they need to stop their abhorrent behavior.

Also helping put a positive end to this particular fray was the fact the rest of the family knew Steve very well. They had a great deal of respect for him and knew that such behavior was not part of his makeup.

Can you imagine the amount of damage something like this could have had? Steve's relationship with this family is one he values very much, and it is one that he could have lost had he not confronted the gossiper head-on.

Now sit back and consider the amount of energy required from everyone, not to mention the uneasiness, in this situation. All the unpleasant crosstalk must have negatively impacted the entire family.

I'd like to make one thing very clear. I mentioned above that confronting the guilty party is usually the best course of action. By confrontation, I'm not referring to the overtly aggressive style of confronting another person. It should not be fraught with beratement or yelling; rather, it should be done in a civil manner. It should be more like a common-sense conversation than the Spanish Inquisition.

So, What's a Family to Do?

Here's another story I heard from James, another associate of mine. James told me he'd had a string of conversations with members of his family about gossip.

One of the elder family members said, "If we don't gossip, then what else will we have to talk about?"

Jim told me he just looked dubiously at the man waiting for a further explanation. The old man was quite serious in his question. What would they do if they couldn't talk about other people, meaning to gossip and spread rumors? It was obviously a mainstay of their family culture.

In my travels, I've noticed the lack of entertainment seems to be a reality in certain societies around the world. I've often thought the lack of media availability and external stimulation were the root causes of this phenomenon.

More and more, however, I have observed that a

significant percentage of this kind of toxic behavior – using gossip as a form of entertainment – is cultural. In such situations, it's a pastime parents pass on to their children. At an early age, children adopt the behavior as being appropriate. They are affirmed in this belief because everyone else around them is doing it.

In most modern societies, a significant part of healthy interpersonal interaction gets its start in teaching children from a very early age to communicate clearly and directly. Wise people want to teach the next generation to be open and honest when communicating with others.

My 90–10 Rule

Although the nature of gossip varies between different families and workplaces, I have often seen it break down like this: gossip is roughly 10% about what actually happened and 90% about the speaker's interpretation and reaction.

Think about that for a minute. Seem about right to you?

Consider the outcome of Exercise #1. How much personal interpretation was infused into the story as it passed from person to person?

The 90–10 rule is certainly not limited to any particular society. I see that trend going on in the United States as well as many other cultures. Personal biases, rumors and innuendos have become important components of our communication structure.

As if by osmosis, parents wittingly or unwittingly put these components in the communication "toolboxes" of their children. These components, along with the art of gossip itself get passed down from generation to generation.

It Doesn't Improve with Age

As people grow older, the tendency to gossip often becomes stronger and stronger. It becomes so deeply ingrained in people, they are no longer able to notice there is anything wrong with it. They have been raised to think that this is simply the way they and everyone else communicate and that there's nothing that can be done about it.

Even people who do notice the negative aspects of gossiping typically don't know what to do about it. Both gossips and gossip victims usually remain clueless and simply go on their merry way.

The natural acceptance of gossip as an intractable fact of life is what causes gossips to keep gossiping. Gossip victims often feel they are helpless to do anything about the situation. Sure, they get angry and try to fight back, but to whom do they slap with a rebuttal when the gossip chain becomes so dispersed?

Too often, gossip victims hold their upset feelings inside since they don't know how to fight this faceless enemy in the shadows. Their ill feelings fester and their resentment grows, while they sit back in hopes the storm will pass and normality will return.

The best solution I can offer at this point is one that was included in one of the stories I related earlier. Whenever possible, identify the original source of the gossip and confront that person. Having a stern and frank discussion with the gossip originator may be the only out for the victim.

In upcoming chapters, we'll examine other methods of handling this problematic situation.

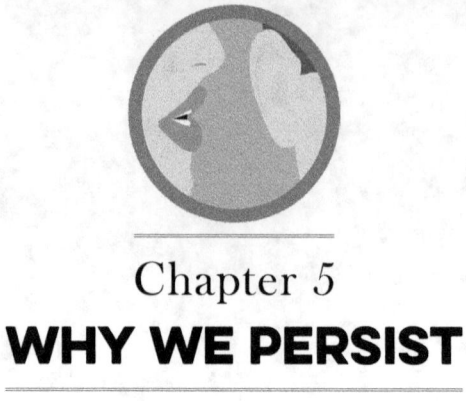

Chapter 5
WHY WE PERSIST

"We first make our habits, then they make us."
—John Dryden

So, why do so many of us persist in gossiping even when we realize it's not a healthy habit?

Understanding this is going to require some deep thinking. It takes lots of courage and commitment to see the truths involved here. Most importantly, it requires a great deal of willingness to begin to see things about ourselves we may not want to see.

Think of it as a layer of your personality you could not see before. If you are willing to go there and confront a truth about yourself, I promise you a miracle could happen as a result of what you see.

Let's look at some of the common reasons why gossip is so juicy, so you can see for yourself what it is that's so appealing. If you take this information as a signal for positive change, I promise it will make a huge difference for you in both your personal and professional life.

.... **Exercise #2 – Why Do You Gossip?**

If you are in a group setting, pair up with a partner. If you are reading this book alone, you can do this exercise by yourself. However, it is more effective with a partner.

First, ask your partner (or yourself) to tell you about a juicy bit of gossip in their life. Give them about three minutes or so. Then you take your turn telling a bit of your own gossip.

After you have heard each other's gossip, ask the other person "Why do you gossip?" Then ask yourself "Why do I gossip?" This conversation will allow you to really discover something about why it is that people gossip, including yourself.

Listen closely for justifications from the other person. Do they derive enjoyment from gossip? Be honest about how you justify gossiping and the degree to which you enjoy it.

Next, have a conversation about how you feel after gossiping, whether you're the one who initiated it or you're merely passing it along.

From all the discussions I've had over the years concerning how people have felt after being involved in gossiping, the overwhelming majority has expressed some degree of guilt after the fact.

I found the degree of guilt ranges on the spectrum anywhere from a bothersome twinge of guilt to feeling miserable about the part they played. The more guilt or misery a person feels about being a gossip, the higher the odds they will be able to stop the behavior.

A large percentage of the population feel no guilt about being a gossip. Most of these people even get a morbid sense of enjoyment from it. At the risk of coming across overly harsh, the term "sociopath" comes to mind when thinking about this latter group.

…….. **End of Exercise**

Now that we've discussed some key dynamics of the gossiping mechanism, let's consider several of the most common reasons people gossip. Keep in mind the list of reasons below is not all-inclusive. This is a summary of the most common reasons I have heard from people over the years. The list is also not mutually exclusive in that some situations may involve a blending of two or more reasons.

The Need to Play the Victim

One very common reason people initiate gossip about others comes from a desire to play the victim in a given situation. Many people call this the "oh, poor me" syndrome.

Typically, when people are wronged they feel hurt. Many who feel hurt get the urge to strike back. What better way to strike back than to spread nasty rumors about them to people they know?

One example that comes to mind is the breakup of a love relationship. When a person who is romantically involved with someone gets the unexpected or at least unwanted news from his or her partner that they want to end the relationship, things can get ugly.

After the tears and harsh words subside, the victim of the breakup may want to strike back. The need to "get even" may seem to them like a great justification for spreading nasty gossip about their ex-partner. The gossip may be in the form of a made-up lie or a truth that should otherwise be kept in confidence.

The Need to Be Right

As humans, we are all driven to avoid being wrong. Even when we may have some doubts, the desire to be right about almost everything seems to be part of our DNA.

Whenever we're trying to get others to believe us, to agree with us, to take our side, or even to feel sorry for us, being right about what we claim is usually of utmost importance. Our inner voice is always telling us we must prevail, even if logic or other factors suggest we might just be wrong. OMG, perish the thought!

As soon as we take a stand that we're right – at any cost – someone or something else must automatically be wrong. Consider this. What is the true cost of always having to be right? The emotional cost … the reputation cost … the relationship cost. Before putting your stake in the ground, take a deep breath, ponder the costs, and then articulate your position.

It takes a lot of courage for someone to admit his or her burning need to be right, but the pathway to altering any relationship for the better is by taking of responsibility for your actions.

Here's a story about being right that you may find both interesting and helpful:

A few years ago, I was speaking with a relative of mine who was struggling with his overwhelming need to always be right ... even when his inner voice was telling him there was a chance he was wrong. He realized this behavior could be a bit self-destructive but didn't know how to let go of the habit.

I asked him if he had ever heard the story of the monkeys and the bananas. He said that he had not so I shared the following true story with him:

In a certain part of Asia, people have a particular way of capturing monkeys. They build a large square or rectangular box that has clear thick plastic on all sides. The plastic has holes in the sides that are designed so that a monkey can squeeze its hand in to grab one of the bananas that have been placed inside the box as bait. No matter how hard the monkeys try, they are not able to get even a single banana out while holding on to it.

Once the trappers place these banana-filled traps at the bottom of a hill, they sit on the hill to wait and watch.

One by one, monkeys come down to the box and put their hands inside to grab a banana. Even though they're unable to extract a prized banana, they become entrenched in the effort. They will not let go of the banana. They hold onto it as if their life depends on it, even though, if they let go of that banana, they can be free. The monkey trapper comes down and captures the stuck monkeys.

The monkeys remain with their hands stuck in the box since they are sure they are right about their ability to secure a banana. The monkeys are so stubborn about being right in their pursuit, they become easy prey for the trappers.

After relating this story, I asked my relative to consider that human beings behave in a very similar way. When we are convinced we are right about something, we are just like the monkeys, unwilling to let go, holding on tighter and tighter as though our life depends on it.

Similar to the conundrum faced by the monkeys, many humans fail to realize the solution is quite simple. If we let go, we will be free. In the case of us humans, the trappers are our own emotions.

The Urge to Complain

Imagine, for just a moment, what life would be like if all human beings practiced the art of thinking carefully before speaking or acting. Wow, what a concept!

For those of you who have never felt the need to complain about something, please close the book now.

OK, great. You're all still here.

There is absolutely nothing wrong with complaining. We all do it when faced with unpleasant situations. Again, there is a spectrum of complainers here ... from the casual complainers who seldom get their feathers ruffled to the chronic complainers who see negatives almost every time they turn around.

I know some of you are wondering about the correlation between complaining and gossiping.

So, here it is.

Complaints cover a multitude of sins – anywhere from relationship problems, defective products, poor service, people who rub us the wrong way, or people we simply do not like.

The last two reasons above represent the most likely cases where we have a direct link between complaining and gossiping. I have already addressed the concept of confronting people with whom we have a disagreement and that applies here as well.

People who lack the skill for civil confrontation or simply do not care to address an unpleasant situation head-on have two basic options:

1. Keep the complaint to themselves and do nothing, or
2. Complain to others, which usually falls under the gossip category.

When gossiping about the complaints we have with other people, we naturally include our justifications for being upset and throw in some "color commentary" to support our position. We naturally want to paint ourselves as being in the right and the other party as being in the wrong. If there are mitigating factors that might suggest any fault of our own, we'll most likely leave such details out of the conversation. Sound a little one-sided? In fact, it is – and that's the nature of the majority of gossip.

The juicier we make our story and the more condescending our tone, the more we invalidate the target of our gossip. And the more frequently we tell the story to other gossip partners, the more we convince ourselves that it is 100% true.

It does not take long before the serious gossiper becomes so enamored with their own story, they lose sight of the harm it is doing to the victim. They cannot see the harm they are inflicting because they have wrapped themselves in a cocoon of sorts. I use the word cocoon because a person's justifications get so thick that they cannot see outside of them.

The gossiper's unwillingness or inability to confront the target of their gossip becomes a defense mechanism and their cocoon becomes an effective firewall. They will avoid such a confrontation for fear that they and/or their story will be invalidated when and if new facts surface to support the position of the gossip victim.

The Desire to Feel Superior

Closely related to the need to be right is the desire to feel superior to the gossip target and perhaps even to many of those in the gossip chain.

The gossiper with this superiority complex wants to be seen as the "top dog" within his or her sphere of influence.

It not only makes them look good amongst their peers, it makes them feel good about themselves.

This scenario manifests itself in the form of arrogance. Those who get caught up in it will go out of their way to make up lies and build on previous stories with more tall tales to bolster their own popularity.

Looking good is a big deal for lots of people. The flip side – not looking bad – is equally big. People will generally not be proactive when it comes to such avoidance until such time as they hear some negative gossip about themselves.

Gossipers caught up in this trap often regret what they have done or said. However, the justification for their position is much stronger than their desire to resolve any conflict it causes.

The Need to Be in Control

Another reason a person gossips is that it gives them a certain power. It provides them with the sensation of being in control, even if it's only momentary. It means they can dominate the situation or even the other person.

These "control freaks" may not see themselves as domineering. They're probably OK with adjectives such as self-righteous or even sanctimonious, but they don't want to be labeled as domineering due to its more negative connotations. Sorry folks, I call it like I see it, plain and simple: domineering.

Why? Because they are the ones who created the gossip

blast in the first place, and they put forth substantial effort to control any and all interpretations of the story. Since the gossiper is talking behind the other person's back, realistically there is no way the targeted victims can defend themselves. This automatically makes them the controlled party – the loser.

Control and dominance are also elements that will enhance the gossiper's sense of their own value. When we dominate, we do not realize that we will do everything to prevent the other person from turning the tables and playing the domination game themselves.

If you were to ask the gossiper if he or she sees themselves as domineering, their response would almost invariably be "No. Who am I dominating?"

Perhaps without realizing it as such, they are assuming the dominant position by controlling the conversation and positioning themselves as the righteous leader. Taking that position justifies their statements and actions.

Chapter 6
LISTEN MORE; YOU'LL GOSSIP LESS

"Most of the successful people I've known are the ones who do more listening than talking."

—Bernard Baruch

So far, I've concentrated mostly on gossip as it passes verbally from one person or group to the next. After all, gossiping is primarily about talking.

I'd like to shift gears and look at the other side of the coin, listening. In modern society, I truly believe we have lost the art of listening. Of course, that assumes we had perfected that art at some point.

Like many others, I believe listening is the most important element of communication. Often people who gossip simply did not truly comprehend what they were told, or at least did not get it accurate.

People hearing gossip take what they thought they

heard, add interpretations and possibly their own biases to it, and then re-share with others. In the Twitter world, this is called a re-tweet, but we'll get to that later. The cycle goes on. Pretty soon, you've got a soap opera in the works!

Listening and Relationships

If you look closely at your relationships, you will see that the effectiveness of your relationships is determined by how well you communicate. How well you communicate with others is determined, by and large, by how well you listen.

The well-known leadership expert Steve Shapiro puts it this way:

"Low quality of relationships = Low quality of life and High quality of relationships = High quality of life."

Listening is the key ingredient of relationships. I call it the secret sauce of all successful relationships.

We have all likely been in a situation when someone has said to us, "You don't listen."

Often our response is to say, "Oh yes, I was listening."

Consider that in many of those cases, however, it is actually true that we were not listening.

What were we doing then?

First, let's distinguish listening from hearing. Hearing is

physical. You could be playing with your phone, writing or doing something else while someone else is talking and still hear them. You will capture part of what they are saying, but not everything. Most importantly, you won't absorb their core meaning.

The reason for this is that we have a secondary voice. Let's call this voice the small voice or monkey chatter.

Freed dictionary defines this secondary voice as "an inner voice that judges your behavior, voice of conscience, wee small voice."

The Urban dictionary definition is: "That voice in your head that says do it, food, internet, music, name, religion, sex, sports, work. I really want this, but don't have the money, should I steal it?"

That small voice is talking all the time. As a matter of fact, that secondary voice is talking while you are reading this book.

This small voice will tell you how to read the book that is open in front of you right now. It will influence how you think, what you should do and what you shouldn't do.

That little chattering voice is continuously talking. It continues even when someone else is talking. Your mind goes where the small voice takes it, and therefore, you're far from present.

Proper Listening Takes Practice

Listening is a habit. Like any other habit, it will take some practice to alter it. First, let's take a look at what listening is not.

Listening is not automatically responding to someone. It is not you waiting for your chance to get your two cents in or wanting to tell your side of the story immediately. Ever been interrupted in the middle of a sentence? It's not only irritating but it's a signal the other person was not listening – or maybe they were being just plain rude.

If you are able to learn how to listen closely, two things will happen:

1. Your relationship with yourself will alter and you will have much more self-confidence.
2. People will respect you more and your self-respect will improve as well.

People actually see that you are listening and will value the relationship with you much more, since finding a true listener is an unusual occurrence in today's fast-paced world.

Listening is not completing someone's sentence. It is not putting words in their mouth. How often have you found yourself doing that? How do you think the other person feels when you do that?

When there is a break in the other person's talking, don't think you have to open your mouth right away to fill the silent void. Even if you have something to say, pause before you start talking. This usually allows the other person to see that you are thinking carefully about what they have said before you respond. Don't be afraid of the somewhat awkward silence. Have a pensive look on your face. Such actions will solidify the other person's appreciation of your listening skills.

Listening is not giving advice or trying to tell people what to do. You don't need to fix other people's problems. When someone is sharing something important, or something that they are challenged with, they are not looking for your opinion (unless, of course, they ask you for it). You don't have to inject your opinion right away. Wait for your turn in the conversation.

Listening is not telling the person who is right or who is wrong. You do not need to pose as the judge and jury of a situation. By telling a person that he/she is right in a gossip situation, you have inadvertently fueled the gossip chain. In such cases, you've indirectly talked behind the third person's back, whether you meant to or not. That other person has automatically been diminished.

The other thing about listening is that it doesn't need to be all about you. You don't have to relate a story to yourself and make it be about you. When you do that, you are exhibiting selfishness and will lose the other person's respect.

What I have covered so far about listening, if you look at it deeply, is your little chatterer at play. It is about turning the whole conversation into being about you.

I am going to give you some suggestions about how to listen. If you practice them, I promise you it will alter this potentially damaging behavior.

You first must be able to discover for yourself that you are not listening and take full responsibility for that behavior. Becoming aware of this behavior is the first and biggest step to altering your listening.

Eye contact is the key. You need to be fully connected with the other person. This does not mean staring at them, but actually listening with your brain, your heart and your spirit. Allow yourself to enter the other person's world. If you allow yourself to get that deep, you will start to see something for yourself that you never saw before, both about yourself and about the other person.

The process of listening is continuous. It has to be moment by moment. This means constantly bringing yourself forth, asking yourself the question, "Am I listening? Am I listening to what is being said? Or, am I listening to my small voice?"

The next step is being able to fully comprehend what the other person is saying to you. This might mean stopping the other person to ask clarification questions. "Wait a minute; I want to see if I can repeat what you just said." You repeat what you believe you heard and then check with them to see if you're correct.

In some cases, you may be surprised at what the other person says in response. They may realize what they said was incorrect – maybe a little, maybe a lot – and restate something more accurately.

Practicing this method allows you the ability to listen more keenly. Those pauses to ensure understanding are critical to good conversation.

Also critical in conversations are your periodic acknowledgments of what the other person has said by interjecting words and phrases such as, "really", "wow", "great", "thank you for sharing that", "interesting" and other words or phrases of that nature.

Listening Sets the Stage for the Credibility Test

Still wondering about the linkage between gossiping and listening?

Here it is. A good listener can stop a gossip in his or her tracks.

So, you've been attentive and have actively participated in a conversation with a gossip who has been relating a story to you. You have acknowledged you've listened to what they had to say.

Here's your golden opportunity to validate or invalidate their story. Actually, it's not you who is doing this, it's the gossip themself. All you have to do is ask a few pointed questions at the proper times and the gossip will be forced to take the appropriate action, unless they're simply unwilling to do so and are holding on to being right.

Here's how it will go. At key points in the conversation, the gossip will drop one of their gossip bombs, a juicy tidbit that bolsters one of their main points. This is one of those moments where you might say, "Wow, that's very interesting."

This creates a slight pause in the conversation, and it gives you an opening to more or less challenge the veracity of what they have said.

A simple question like, "And how do you know that to be true?" forces the gossip to either present actual evidence, make up another lie or admit it may not be true. If they can't present the evidence, you have them in a corner.

You can then follow up with: "Well, this sounds like it could be just a rumor, and I'm certainly not going to repeat it. If I were you, I'd be very careful with this story. If it's not true and it gets around that you're spreading unfounded rumors about ******, it could come back to bite you."

Regardless of the outcome, you have set yourself up as a person of high moral character. As a bonus, you may have stopped a nasty piece of gossip from getting started. And it's all due to being a smart listener.

Reducing Gossip in Circulation

This kind of listening and establishing credibility will further strengthen relationships, and across-the-board strong relationships will reduce the amount of gossip in circulation.

It also reduces the odds of blindly entering a gossip cycle. Why? Because when you're listening, you are in the present moment. You are really hearing what the other person has to say. You're avoiding the temptation to add observations and editorialize.

You listened. You thanked them for valuing you and sharing their thoughts with you. You commented or gave your opinion only when asked for it, leaving the other person with the rewarding experience of being heard.

Your desire to be right or to avoid being wrong or to offer justifications has not entered into the conversation.

This does not mean you have to agree with everything the other person has said. Healthy debate is ... well, healthy ... as long as it is civil in tone. It will often stop ugly gossip before it builds up a head of steam.

If you reach this higher plateau of listening, I promise you will feel great about yourself. And, people with whom you are interacting will have greater respect for you. It will greatly reduce the intra-family squabbles I alluded to earlier.

On a more global basis, adopting a higher quality of listening will probably resolve many of the societal problems we face today.

We have inherited the practice of not listening. Until we become fully responsible for our contribution to that, nothing will alter.

.... Exercise #3 – Stop Listening

In a group setting, find a partner. Sit face to face. One partner will be "A" and the other partner will be "B".

Partner A will share something important in her/his life. It is partner B's responsibility to do anything but listen. They can show this by looking at their phone, looking into their purse to find something, taking their shoes off, scratching their head or picking their nose (I know, gross but effective). The objective is to do anything except to listen.

You will do this for about forty-five seconds to a minute.

Now switch roles and repeat the same exercise. This is to be sure that both participants get a good sense of what it feels like when someone is not listening.

Now a good question to ask would be, how was it for each one of you?

What do you think about the impact?

This will give both partners a good idea of what it feels like when someone is not listening, especially when you have something important to say.

Next, Partner A is going to share again and this time Partner B is really going to listen. They are going to be fully present for what the other person is saying.

This will also go for about forty-five seconds to a minute. Partner B will share and repeat the same exercise.

After you have each taken a turn, discuss how the experience was for each of you? What was it like when someone was truly listening to you?

This exercise brings awareness to how much we actually do not listen and how fundamental it is to work on our listening.

……. **End of Exercise**

Being in the Present

Improving our listening skills means learning to stay in the present during our conversations with others. We must not let our inner chatterer force us off course. There is only one exception to this:

Sometimes our inner chatterer will remind us of a previous incident or piece of knowledge that falls into the "lessons learned" category. If that thought content has a *direct* bearing on the current conversation, it's better not to ignore it. It should probably be interjected into the conversation. When and how that should be done is highly situational and needs to be executed with care.

Let me give you an example: If you were in an abusive relationship and you ended that relationship, the incidents of that abuse would be stored in your memory. Your small voice will remind you of those stories in your memory and will prevent you from getting close to someone new, or a lot of the time, you will be resigned to have a conversation with someone to create a new relationship.

Poor listening behaviors are not something that we are born with. They develop over time based on family values (or lack thereof), education, environmental situations and cultural issues.

Fixing such negative behaviors is part of the maturing process. We should realize, like it or not, that process is not a single event but a continuous journey.

Chapter 7
TECHNOLOGY: GOSSIP'S NEW FRONTIER

"Technological progress has merely provided us with more efficient means for going backwards."

—Aldous Huxley

It's not surprising news to anyone that technology has advanced by staggering leaps and bounds in the last generation.

When I was a young man growing up, there was at least one landline telephone in most houses. There was also a phone booth on most street corners just in case you had to make a call when away from home.

Technology has not only led to the demise of the venerable phone booth (sorry, Superman, you'll have to find a new changing room), it's led to a complete reinvention of how we communicate.

Today, not only do most of us carry a powerful phone

booth in our pocket but those mobile phones, almost surgically attached to us, give us instantaneous access to a worldwide network of information and much more. Often that "much more" can be more negative than positive.

Most of us who precede the Millennial generation agree that in spite of all the tremendous benefits, the explosive reliance on the internet and cyberspace has severely damaged the quality of people's face-to-face communication skills.

Gamers, hackers and other introverts can now live in their parents' basements for days or weeks without seeing the light of day or needing to communicate directly with other human beings.

For many people, texting has made talking to others obsolete. Whereas the tongue used to be among the most powerful muscles in the human body, thumbs are on the rise to challenge that position.

A person can say a lot without ever really saying it directly. And it's not just texting that has taken over a good bit of the communication network. Social media platforms such as Facebook, Instagram and Twitter have given rise to faceless communication. Whereas texting requires two-way interaction, social media platforms provide open forums where one-way tirades can be transmitted to millions around the world instantaneously.

People often ask me if what gets posted on social media platforms should be considered gossip?

Well, let's take a closer look at this

Forgetting for a moment the limits some platforms have placed on content, social media is rather democratic. A person has a profile or a page, and they can post whatever they want on it – an update on their job search, a picture of their child, or an article about what their favorite sports team is up to this season. Few things are off-limits. An amazing amount of obscenity and pornography are either outright allowed or slip through the platform filters regularly.

Part of what makes social media more complicated is that sharing, by and large, goes out to everyone following that person's profile and sometimes beyond authorized followers. It might be your boss, your child's teacher or an old high school friend. If you're on the list to follow that person, you follow everything. And when it comes to someone reposting your content, all bets are off.

If someone posts a story about himself or herself or about a consenting member of their social-media circle, it's fair game. The subject could be anything in their life or the lives of their friends or followers. The audience has no control over that content. Since that person has decided to post a particular story, they ostensibly have given permission to all their followers to know about it for whatever reason.

If a social-media post involves information about where someone went on vacation or that one of their children just graduated from high school, it's almost never considered to be gossip.

On the other hand, if someone posts a story about another person that is negative, our view begins to change. If they post a negative story or comment about an entity, a group of people, or any individual other than themself it is most likely considered to be gossip. Notable exceptions are things such as political opinions.

For instance, concerned citizens who post negative comments about President Trump's actions concerning immigration cannot be considered gossip; they're merely public opinion. Even juicy tidbits about Trump's extramarital affairs cannot be considered genuine gossip since he is a public figure. That's more like something one would find in a Hollywood gossip column, which is not the variety of gossip we're discussing here.

Other than the above exceptions, why do we consider negative commentary to be gossip?

Such negative utterances are intended to put someone else down, or as is commonly said, to "throw them under the bus," though I fail to see why that particular vehicle was chosen for this analogy. Perhaps a steamroller would be a better choice?

The person posting such gossip typically has some mean-spirited motivation in their mind when they post. Remember that gossip does not need to be untrue to be considered gossip. Usually, the gossiper is upset, perhaps jealous or simply disagrees with the targeted victim. Oftentimes, gossip is the quickest way to get others on your side with regard to a particular incident and have them feel sympathy for you.

Technology and social media have made almost everything immediately accessible to us. Our resulting reach to the masses imbues us with a false sense of importance. For the first time in human history, we can instantly reach audiences numbering into the thousands (or tens or hundreds of thousands) as easily as pulling a lightning-fast device out of our back pocket.

That inflated sense of self-importance allows us to feel righteous. It gives us an uneasy feeling of permission to seek empathy anywhere, while at the same time publicly harming another person or group.

We already have covered extensively why, in general, a person would engage in gossip. What makes social media more ominous is that once a person reads that post, the cycle does not end there. Unlike a rumor spread over the dining table or office coffee pot, the post lasts forever, and any comments attached to it do as well.

Then comes "sharing" a post, another insidious way to spread gossip to further reaches of a social media platform. A person can take that post and share it with someone else, and another and another … and now the cycle of gossip broadens and becomes even more damaging than before.

In summary, you could view social media as one of the best and most efficient tools for enhancing and promoting gossip.

If you are reading this book and you have been involved in this pattern of behavior, I urge you to stop now that you know how damaging it can be. Those who do not stop such behavior are creating a massive, permanent record of their pettiness. Imagine the impact on society. It's staggering.

Chapter 8
GOSSIP'S IMPACT

"Fire and swords are slow engines of destruction, compared to the tongue of a Gossip."

—Richard Steele

Now that we've got our gossip foundation built, let's take a look at the impacts gossip can have on us and those around us.

The Illusion of Satisfaction and Fulfillment

Have you ever wondered about the impact of holding a grudge and of gossiping to others because of it? Consider specifically a case where this concerns a particular person in your life such as a close friend or relative.

It should not require a great deal of thought. All you have to do is allow yourself to become aware of how you are feeling in the midst of all that drama. Is gossip making you more satisfied with your life? You might say, "I get a satisfaction out of being right, and my gossiping allows me to be the winner."

In reality, you're probably feeling just the opposite inside. If you're like most people, you probably feel no true sense of satisfaction or fulfillment from gossiping. Instead, you may be making yourself a bit miserable over the harm you've caused.

If you think I am full of it, I challenge you to go ahead and look inside your heart. What is really going on in there?

Is there satisfaction? Is there any fulfillment?

No Longer Feeling Love for Yourself or Others

This is one impact of gossip that unfortunately gets completely ignored.

When we find ourselves wrapped up in that kind of twisted, unhealthy behavior, our attention becomes focused on proving ourselves right. We want to be in control of the situation and to be in the right.

Where does that put love?

When we engage in gossip, we automatically throw out any sense of love and affinity. Our affections and compassion go right out the window. The really distressing fact is that we do not see this in relation to ourselves, the other person, or even other people around us.

Gossip precludes the emotion of love. It pollutes our vision until we cannot see the forest for the trees. This becomes the case even when someone brings it to our attention.

Why does gossip interfere so directly with love?

Gossip consumes our necessary faculties for love. We become so terribly wrapped in our own petty agendas that we become blind about what it is doing to our body, mind and relationships.

I want you to go ahead and honestly ask yourself: When this kind of behavior is going on, am I loving myself? Am I honoring myself and life in general? Am I honoring my promises toward others, especially the person I am gossiping about?

Putting a Gag on Our Self-Expression

The impact of gossip on our capacity for self-expression can be unreal.

How often do people find themselves trapped, feeling that they cannot say what they need to say? How common is it that they share what troubles they are dealing with, their complaints about another person or what is happening to them?

Why is this so common?

The main reason is that there is some other internally oriented conversation going on below the surface. This is a conversation that encourages the person to go into their shell and withhold their feelings.

Let's say you are upset with someone. Now picture your inner chatterer inside your brain saying, "Do not talk to that person."

What do you do? You will very often turn to a third party, a person you perhaps trust deeply (or maybe someone you don't trust at all) and express your complaint, upset feelings or dissatisfaction with the other person.

That feeling of being upset has now graduated to the state of gossip. What will the person to whom you're gossiping do with your story? Perhaps they will go tell someone else, which creates a gossip chain and you have no control over where that leads. But at least you've gotten it off your chest which provides some temporary relief.

The alternative to venting your feelings to another person is to keep your emotions to yourself. Keeping them bottled up inside yourself creates a problem of a different sort. It's almost impossible to find a win-win solution here.

So, let's say you decide to take the high road, refrain from gossiping about the incident and hold the hurt inside. This hides your feelings from the people who are close to you, even people you love. Those people will sense there is something wrong because hiding one's feelings almost always creates a degree of withdrawal. Close friends and family will see you're not the "whole" person you normally are.

You might want to look back at your past for a minute. Do you recall any incidents where you said to yourself, "I'm not going to express my feelings on this because I don't want to get hurt again" or "I don't want to experience this type of incident again"?

If your answer is yes, then you know what is triggering your thoughts is not the present situation. Instead, it's simply a blast from the past. What has happened in the past is just that, it's the past and that's behind you. Realizing this is a warning to not let it happen again is positive.

This does not mean, however, that you should do nothing. If you look at the situation objectively, it could very well be an opportunity for self-expression. This breaks the gossip pattern and you're no longer a prisoner of your own emotions.

Don't Bury Your Feelings

There are many times when people know they are keeping hurt feelings inside, missing the chance to tell others how they really feel. Expressing your feelings can set you free and change your outlook. Burying your true feelings may be a deeply ingrained behavior from your past. Buried feelings usually come out naturally and we don't know how to stop this from happening.

A very powerful thing to do, when confronted with the issue of gossip in your life, is to recognize that you are about to go into your cocoon, giving in to your misguided justifications. Before you slip into that cocoon, shake it off and get back into the present moment.

Allow yourself to become aware of the impact of not expressing your feelings. Until you embrace the present moment with crystal clarity, you will not be able to stop the negative chatter going on in your head.

If you don't recognize that you are being driven by your little chatterer and events from the past, and you continue that behavior, you are nothing but a prisoner.

Draining Your Health and Liveliness

Based on all my years of education, research and working with clients, I can promise you one thing for certain …

Setting yourself up as a staunch gossip will damage your health and well-being.

The need to always be in the right regardless of situational realities and to have full command of all the justifications you use for your actions result in a severe mental drain. That constant mental strain takes its toll on your health over time.

If you take a moment to think about it, what do you think gossip is doing to your precious health and vitality? Do you really believe it's doing nothing?

I have news for you. Gossip is not health neutral.

Gossiping is probably one of the most destructive things a human being can do to the body. It's another one of those silent killers, since people who do it regularly don't realize the harm they're doing to themselves.

I realize this may sound outrageous. It's widely accepted that things like alcohol, drugs, stress and tobacco are health hazards. But gossip? How can that be hazardous to your health? As an expert on the subject who has studied this carefully for many years, I can state it as a fact.

There is a detrimental physical impact on our body when we withhold our feelings. A lack of honest expression to the person who has upset or disappointed us can ravage our body from the inside out. It's like stress, only worse. For almost everyone, this source of stress is a major blind spot.

Why Is That the Case?

When a person becomes wrapped up in their own self-righteousness, they have every justification to defend their position regardless of the reality of the situation. Denying this urge creates the blind spot.

If someone brings your core problem to your attention, you will very likely defend your position, tooth and nail. You will try your best to convince that person he or she is wrong and that you are right.

The End Effect Is That Gossip Is Killing You

When you start to take a deeper look at gossip and its effects, you will realize this is true. That state of mind where you cannot see anything except your point of view is a very toxic place to be in.

If you engage in gossip more than you should, I challenge you to take a deep look at the situation. What do you think this pattern of gossiping is doing to you? Is there anything lively or uplifting about the situation?

Is there anything at all that seems to matter except, of course, your point of view?

Reading this book from cover to cover is a great way

to fully understand what gossiping behavior is actually doing to you.

I am willing to wager that you, as a normal human being, may very well choose to turn to gossip as a way out when you have a complaint about someone in your life. Unfortunately, it's in our nature. But that doesn't mean it has to stay there. If it's not exorcised, it can seriously damage your state of mind, and ultimately your health.

My expert opinion is that when you're engaged in gossip, you are not your true self.

Extreme Cases Have Dire Results

In severe situations, malicious gossip can be disastrous. In such cases, there is no love. There is no passion or compassion for anything else in the world.

Simply put, there is no aliveness. Yet, in a strange way, you may actually be getting a sort of morbid enjoyment out of gossiping.

You are probably now saying to yourself that this conclusion is quite disgusting. You're right. It is.

But when you are wrapped up in that endless cycle of dishonesty and righteousness, you are not being true to yourself or others around you.

What is worse in these extreme situations is that you will do whatever you have to do to prove that everything is right, according to you.

Case in Point

Here is an actual story an associate related to me. This associate is a coach and a therapist. He was attending a gathering at a friend's home in another city. When he arrived at the gathering, there were already about ten people milling about. As the evening progressed, a few more people showed up, making the total about twenty.

Upon his arrival, he was greeted with loving hospitality. Some of the people in attendance that night had been to his previous seminars. Still others, he had coached as his clients. Even though the room was filled with a deep feeling of generosity, love and gratitude, it was a little tense. He sensed that something negative might have happened before his arrival.

Since he is a therapist and sometimes prone to over sensitivity, he realized sometimes when he had this type of feeling in the past, he had been proven wrong. He hoped this was the case that evening.

As he mingled with the other guests, he observed some telltale behaviors signaling something was amiss. As he engaged in conversations with the other guests, he heard things that made him uneasy.

Eventually, he went to the restroom. On the way back to the living room, he walked by the kitchen where the host was cleaning up and preparing more tea. The host confided in him, "I need to talk with you about what happened earlier."

My friend's internal alarm went off, and he said he would

talk to him the next day and then returned to the party. The evening ended on a positive note that made him feel more comfortable. After all, there had been lots of lively conversation and tasty food.

The next day my friend met with the host. As it turned out, he wanted some one-on-one coaching about what had happened the night before.

The host explained that one of the guests at the party had complained about a broken picture frame on the wall. My friend failed to see what all the fuss was about, but the guest had made quite a scene. He kept going on and on, pressing the host about why he would have a broken frame on the wall when he had guests coming over.

The host and his family got upset over the guest's tirade. They gave in and took the framed picture off the wall. However, the incident did not end there.

The host and his family continued to whisper in the kitchen about the complaining guest and his actions and their assumptions about what had caused the unusual behavior. This gossip about the guest continued long after everyone left. The host complained he was exhausted.

My friend provided the man with appropriate coaching. He encouraged him to reach out directly to this guest and get to the bottom of the conflict.

Here's what my friend learned about the impact of the incident:

- The guest who was critical was quiet after his tantrum for most of the night.
- There was a great deal of unresolved tension in the room.
- The host and his family were upset the entire evening.
- They avoided any direct conversations with all of the guests.
- Obviously, the complaining guest was upset and could not wait to get out of there.
- There were feelings of unease and substantial stress on all participants.

This is a simple, easy-to-track example of how gossip starts and what happens when it festers. Most likely, the aftermath of this incident would have dragged on had the host not had the conversation with the therapist. What would have transpired among this group of people going forward?

As it turned out, the host eventually had a conversation with the unruly guest. The guest admitted he had been in the wrong and made a few excuses about what caused him to act the way he did. He promised that this would not happen again.

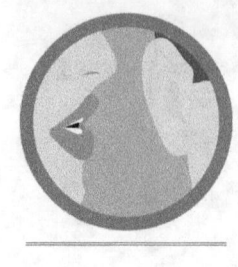

Chapter 9
MOTIVATION TO STOP GOSSIPING

"Good character going bad is like a beast escaping its cage; it will be hard to capture it again!"

—Israelmore Ayivor

One of the most powerful ways to motivate yourself to alter a behavior is to have someone else hold you accountable. This can be scary.

When you have someone else holding you accountable, there is less room for slipping or sliding in your resolve. Instead, you're focused on accomplishing your goal.

We have been talking about gossip, and by now, it must be crystal clear to you that gossip is a behavior. With the right incentive, almost all of us can change our behavior. Having someone hold you accountable to do some of the exercises in this book will assure success, alteration and transformation.

MOTIVATION TO STOP GOSSIPING

.... **Exercise #4 – A Mental Mulligan**

Here is another powerful exercise:

Before going to bed at night, visualize a situation from your day. Choose one where you have reacted in a certain unsavory way, like gossiping for example.

What would have been the proper way that you could have responded or reacted that would have improved the outcome? If your answer is the same as what you did that day, close your eyes, take a deep breath and allow yourself to calm down. When you experience calmness, then ask yourself the question again. If your answer didn't change, choose a different situation.

However, if you come to the conclusion that your original response was appropriate, please consider this before dismissing the situation in question: Was your need to be right so strong that you were like the monkey who could not let go of the banana?

If you're like most of us, you did come up with at least one incident where your behavior was not as you'd have liked it to be. There are times all of us would like to have a "do over," or in golfing terms, "a mulligan." Well, at least mentally, you just got one!

.... **End of Exercise**

Here is another story that an associate related to me. To keep things anonymous, we'll call him Ted.

Over a holiday, Ted traveled to Florida to visit several

members of his extended family. His trip was a welcome respite from the cold of Michigan where he lived.

One of his family members, let's call her Joyce, had recently been upset with another relative who lived nearby. Just for kicks, we'll call him Bill. Ted had heard a little about this rift from previous conversations. Joyce claimed that she was not terribly upset, but that she simply did not want to continue any sort of relationship with Bill. Even though Ted expected to hear more about this conflict over the holiday, he did not. But, it was still an unpleasant way to start his trip to Florida.

He could tell that Joyce's brash statement was bothersome to her. Holding this kind of a grudge is hard on a person. He could see she was not at peace with her decision.

After a few days, Ted suggested they should get together with Bill to celebrate the holiday. He made no mention of wanting to help mend fences, but she refused the idea anyway. She said no, straight out.

Ted respected her wishes even though he knew there was no way she could be at peace with herself. Since he loved the whole family and wanted peace between them, it kept bothering him.

Then he ended up spending a couple of nights in the nearby town where Bill lived with his family. In confidence, Bill expressed a strong desire to have a reconciliation conversation with Joyce. The rift had caused both him and his immediate family a great deal of stress.

Ted listened closely to what Bill was saying and watched

his facial expressions as he talked. Ted waited for a break in the conversation where he could slip in a suggestion without seeming manipulative.

Ted calmly laid out his idea to Bill. "When I get back over to Joyce's house, why don't you call me there. I'll make it seem like an innocent call. After we chat a bit, I'll call Joyce over and hand her the phone."

After a few days, Bill took the leap and called. When Ted approached Joyce with the phone, she steadfastly refused and said she did not want to talk to Bill. After a little friendly nudge from Ted, she reluctantly took the phone.

As they started talking, Joyce's husband became enraged with Ted. He stormed about the house. He got really upset and started venting his fury directly at Ted. He said Ted should leave them alone and warned him about interfering in their relationships.

"If you continue your meddling," he roared furiously, "you will not be welcome here."

After a tense twenty-minute conversation, Joyce got off the phone. She said that after the talk she felt much calmer and lighter. Talking with Bill, although it did not cure everything, was a first significant step to mending the rift and returning both family members to peace. After the husband cooled off, he could see how much of a difference it made for his wife to have a conversation with Bill.

***

There are several things of note here that are important to mention. These kinds of conflicts might be going on undetected in any family. Do any of the symptoms itemized below sound familiar? If so, it might be time to take action.

- The cycle of gossip has been going on for a few years, with combatants on both sides.
- Neither side for the longest time has wanted to take any kind of responsibility for doing anything about the cycle.
- Each family member prefers having conversations about the rift, but complains to their spouses or parents rather than facing their adversary.
- There appears to be no peace of mind for either party in the dispute.
- Two formerly friendly relatives, who live close to each other, have no relationship. Additionally, the related families are estranged from one another.
- There is no honest self-expression.
- Both parties claim they are right and the other person is wrong.
- Love and affection are lost between the individuals and/or their families.
- Neither party in the conflict is aware of the impact gossip is having on them, the other party or the other members of the extended families.

The ultimate path to resolution may be nothing more than a simple authentic conversation. It requires one party taking responsibility and both parties forming a mutual agreement to continue the dialogue.

Self-expression can do amazing things for human beings.

For the most part, you know that if you talk about it and hear the other point of view, you will usually become free. Many people, unfortunately, would rather stay in their cocoon and remain isolated. Once a person takes responsibility, peaceful resolutions can happen quickly.

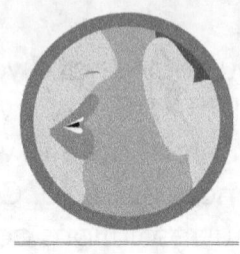

Chapter 10
ENDING THE VICIOUS CYCLE

Gossip behaviors have been around for as long as human beings have inhabited Earth and will most likely continue, in spite of the concerted efforts of books such as this one, unless individuals choose to do something about it.

Although gossip may seem like an unbreakable cultural phenomenon, that view is not entirely correct. Gossip is actually an individual decision. Until the day we as human beings become individually responsible for this destructive behavior, nothing will change.

The only person who can tell you to refrain from gossiping is you. What steps can you take now to help this reality sink in? Here are some recommendations:

- Distinguish or recognize gossip
- Take responsibility to refrain from gossip
- Ask yourself, "Why am I complaining about this person?"
- Ask yourself, "Am I present in this moment?"
- Ask yourself, "What am I listening to right now? Am I listening to my internal chatterer?"
- Ask yourself, "What is the impact of what I am

about to do or say to someone else?"
- Ask yourself, "What am I getting out of doing this?"

Dive deep into your psyche and ask yourself the question, what do I do when …

- things don't go the way I want them to?
- somebody says something I don't like?
- I am reacting to what has happened, or I am reacting to what I am making up?

What are some strategies for dealing with gossip when it inevitably does happen?

- Acknowledge – Admit the fact you are about to gossip when the urge to do so presents itself.
- Let go – Choose to let go of whatever you are upset about or that you need to be right about.
- Take responsibility – There is no one but yourself to hold responsible.
- Express it – Say whatever you need to say in a positive and committed way to the person that might possibly be the target of your gossip.
- Talk to someone you trust before spreading something toxic.
- Create something new – In my opinion, anyone can alter a behavior and create a new relationship with another person, but it takes courage and commitment. Ask yourself, "What would it be like if everything were ideal in this particular relationship?" or "What kind of relationship would I like to see?" Then, have a conversation with the person from that perspective. It will be a new start, but by practicing it, you will eventually master

creating productive relationships.

Gossip is a behavior. That behavior is developed based on our thinking about an incident and how we, at our core, make sense of what happened. Any fictitious story we make up about the event, or any desire we have to prove ourselves to be right, gets created as a function of a negative thought. This negative thought creates negative attitude, and this negative attitude creates negative behavior. As a thought is created and the resulting emotion follows, it has an impact on our thinking and on our body and causes us to react.

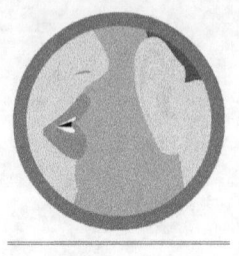

Chapter 11
GOSSIP IN THE WORKPLACE

"Isn't it kind of silly to think that tearing someone else down builds you up?"
—Sean Covey

Imagine this scenario. You walk into the break room on a Monday morning. You notice one of your coworkers, Peter, drinking a cup of coffee. He asks you, "How was your weekend, John?"

You just came out of a great weekend. You had been on a fabulous date with another employee of the company. As a result, you are still excited and on top of the world. You simply cannot help yourself from sharing with your coworker, Peter, what happened. At this point the exchange is not yet gossip.

Part of the reason you choose to share this is to get the other person excited and happy for you. Naturally, you want to feel like your good news is good for others to hear. So, you open your mouth and you spill some of the details of your date. Peter immediately shows excitement for your story. You have been affirmed.

At that particular moment, your life is good. You're a happy camper.

But within a matter of minutes, Peter runs into Joe just down the hall. He shares the story of your date with Joe. Then Peter tells Chris, who is sitting in the next cubicle, who then tells his friend Mark. Because Mark is also seeking some affirmation, he decides to add some stuff that he makes up, before he lets Carl in on the story.

Now, gossip is running rampant!

In a matter of just twenty-four short hours most of the people in the company know something about what happened – true or not true. Consequently, they start looking at both you and your date a little differently. Peter's enthusiasm, it turns out, is not universal.

Both of the employees who have been the subject of the gossip are now embarrassed. You and your date have heard the rumors and you both feel awkward.

The result is both of these employees have been disrespected. The gossip threatens to have a major negative impact on their workplace reputations, and their happiness teeters on the edge of becoming one big disappointment.

***

Here's another scenario:

Consider a larger company, a Fortune 500 corporation that preaches how much they care about their employees. Management and other high-level employees may see the company as having a high level of integrity. The reality, however, may be different than that belief. The company's culture may support an environment that promotes gossip if management does not regularly reinforce the need for behavioral integrity.

Let's look at an example of what can happen in a dysfunctional culture:

Let's say Employee A is growing into the company's leadership structure and is busy doing what is expected of him. Employee B is at a lower level position in the company. He constantly feels jealous of Mr. A.

Mr. B has a close relationship with the company's management. He knows the CEO and reports details of other employees' life situations to the CEO. By allowing such situations to continue, the CEO is acting against his own posture of maintaining good social behavior within the company.

Once Mr. B sees how Mr. A has achieved success, he becomes even more jealous. That jealousy leads him to make up stories and rumors about the rival employee, Mr. A. He takes it upon himself to share these creations with management and the CEO. In a matter of days, gossip is in full spin. In a matter of weeks, the management team starts to pick on Mr. A and within a month, Mr. A is terminated.

This is the ultimate ugly impact of gossip. People's careers or lives get ruined!

If you consider the above scenarios, you'll realize there is never a good outcome from a gossip spiral. A huge amount of time is wasted. Many peoples' reputations are tarnished. Trust and morale are destroyed, and the environment becomes totally polluted. Whole companies with this pattern become destructive places in which many people are unhappy.

It is not an easy job to change an environment of gossip, especially when it is part of a company's culture. Changing it will take time and resources. In my experience, working with companies employing a large number of people, it can take upwards of three to nine months to change the culture. Sometimes even more time is required because it so thick in the culture and the employees keep ignoring the impact.

To alter this behavior requires willingness and commitment.

You may wonder how you can tell the difference between a casual conversation and one that threatens to become gossip. When a casual conversation turns negative, accusatory, or embarrassing to an absent person, it is gossip. This is unhealthy conversation.

Here is how you can tell if a workplace conversation is leading to or becoming gossip:

- The conversation is about someone else and turns into complaints and negativity about the person who is not present.
- The conversation negatively impacts the person

who is the subject (victim), or perhaps the subject is made to appear small.
- The conversation is generated from jealousy and designed to make the gossiper look good. The gossiper or people happy to pass the gossip on to others have a desire to make the subject look bad or incompetent.
- The gossiper does not want to confront the other person, preferring instead to talk to someone else about the juicy details.
- The gossiper does not like what management is doing, but doesn't want to speak to them directly about his or her displeasure.

Often, gossip in the workplace starts with one person. The gossip is talking about the company's future, or how badly management is choosing to handle a certain situation. Perhaps the gossiper is taking issue with inadequate pay or benefits, or something of that nature.

Gossip is the worst when it becomes part of the workplace culture and management chooses to ignore it. What happens then can be dangerously unpredictable. Often management does not know how to handle the gossip, so they just let it go.

At some point, however, usually when things have gotten really bad, they realize that it is starting to destroy the company. If you are on a management team, or in human resources, here are some signs to look for:

- Trusted employees are leaving the company for no apparent reason.
- Employees are taking sides and are divided.

- People are sensitive and seem to be unhappy.
- Employees do not have a great deal of desire to work or even to come to work.
- People start showing up late or slacking off when at their desk.
- There is no trust among employees.
- Productivity has declined.
- There is a troublemaker in the company, someone who is constantly reporting negative news and information about other employees.

Joshua Miller from Learning & Talent Development reports, according to one study conducted by researchers:

- twenty-one percent of employees regularly gossip at work
- fifteen percent of employees occasionally gossip at work
- eighty-six percent of employees gossip about their company
- gossip sessions average fifteen minutes [citation to the study]

These statistics should be alarming. The frequency of gossip is one issue, but consider the loss in productivity. If each gossip conversation takes about fifteen minutes on average, can you imagine how much time is wasted company-wide?

Unfortunately, some people mistakenly believe that gossip is OK or even productive. They cannot comprehend what it would look like if there was no gossip in their environment. Among the chief reasons this is hard for them to see is simply because without gossip, the workplace might seem boring to some folks.

Once gossip becomes a part of the workplace culture, it is much harder for management or other employees to get control over it. If you are in human resources, or are a responsible manager, you should start the rooting out process by having a conversation with each involved person. Next, have a larger meeting with all employees, bringing in a professional coach to work with the entire team. This coach needs to be someone with experience working in dysfunctional business environments.

Chapter 12

COMBATING WORKPLACE GOSSIP

"The world as we have created it is a process of our thinking. It cannot be changed without changing our thinking."

—Albert Einstein

Below is a series of tips and techniques that will help both managers and employees stem the rising tide of gossip-mongering within companies.

Venues for the exchange of gossip can be found in company breakrooms, restaurants that employees frequent, private offices, meeting rooms and so on. And, of course, there's the good old telephone. Now that people have gravitated to the digital era, texting, instant messaging and emails have become the means of communication.

It is important to understand that altering one's behavior, as I have talked about in this book many times, requires a high level of commitment and a willingness to accept change. I highly recommend that you implement these suggestions on how to break the chain of gossip by working on yourself first.

Be a Good Role Model to Others

Being a good role model takes courage and a high degree of discipline. If you hear people gossiping around you, say something like, "Do you understand what you are doing to the person you are gossiping about?" If they don't pay attention to you, walk away and do not engage in any further forms of negative talk or conversation.

Pay More Attention to Your Work

Keep yourself busy on the job and do what is expected of you ... or even better, exceed expectations if you have the skill or energy. If you run out of work and need more to do, ask your supervisor for more. Don't allow yourself to have too much free time on your hands at work.

Be Selective About Workplace Relationships

Finding good friends at work takes time and can be a drawn-out process. It benefits you and your co-workers to take your time and get to know people pretty well before starting to share about your personal life.

Read and Embrace Company Policy

This is quite important for many reasons if one wants to remain employed long-term in a company. It is really important to fully read and understand the company policies and adhere to them. This is especially true of policies concerned with ethical behavior. If your company has a written code of ethics, you'll probably find some anti-gossip rules there. If not, you should consider refraining from gossip to be an unwritten rule.

No Tolerance Policy

If you are forming a company, or working on reviewing policies, it is important to have a no-tolerance policy about gossip. If someone in your employment breaks that policy in the work environment, they should be disciplined. Many people heed the warning to avoid further disciplinary action or termination.

Confront the Gossipers

Confrontation must be done in a light and positive way otherwise you risk deepening the dysfunction. If you are unfortunate enough to be the subject of a chain of gossip, you can say something directly, like, "I have heard such things have been said about me. What do you know about it?" Or, perhaps you can say, "Do you really know that to be true?"

Notify Human Resources of Problems

It is important to let your HR department know about gossip when it happens. That usually means you'll have to divulge the name(s) of the instigator(s). This will take courage since most people do not want to be considered snitches. If you want to have a healthy environment in which to work in, however, you must have the courage to let management know what is going on behind the scenes.

Be Straightforward With Others

Consider straight and to-the-point talk when interacting with managers or your coworkers. Don't beat around the bush if you are uncomfortable as a result of gossip. Say what you have to say directly to the offending person and don't allow fear to get in the way. Co-workers have to understand that you will not tolerate such behavior. They will appreciate you being straight with them instead of gossiping behind their backs.

Encourage the Positive

Having a positive attitude can have a long-lasting effect on a company's culture. The more you practice turning their negatives into positives, the more power you will have. Consequently, you will feel an increased sense of control over yourself by not engaging in any negative conversation that might turn into gossip.

Conduct Employee Guidance Meetings

If you are in management, set up regular meetings to discuss the deeper issues at play within the company. Allow employees to participate by interacting and experiencing the full freedom of self-expression. People must feel trust that they can and should be heard. The more attention you pay, and the more you listen during those meetings, the less chance you have of gossip in the workplace.

Provide Education to Subordinates

To promote a smooth and functional work environment,

you need to provide employees with basic education on human behaviors. If they don't understand what's expected of them, you're just rolling the dice and hoping for the best. You don't need your employees to be psychologists, but they should understand motivations and emotions. With proper behavioral education and proper coaching, once an employee learns to control their outward behavior, they will behave much more positively in the work environment.

Be Careful With Texting and Social Media

Pay close attention to what you are posting on Facebook and other social media channels, and how you phrase things. Keep in mind that typed messages usually come across more bluntly than person-to-person conversation. Think about what you have to say before you say it. Sleep on it before you stick your neck out by taking a certain stand. If you're conflicted, discuss it with your significant other or a trusted friend before you post it.

Deal With the Issue

When you choose to confront a gossip, discuss the core issue of their behavior with them and avoid conversations about their personality. For example, do not say anything about what kind of person they are. Instead say something like, "I am concerned about this gossip and want to see how it can be stopped."

Be Professional at Work

Keeping your private life out of your work environment is sometimes the best way to avoid gossip. Some companies really care about an employee's personal lives and want to help them with their issues. In general, however, be cautious and responsible about what you share with people and how you share it.

Focus on the Solution

Most people focus on describing problems rather than trying to solve them. If you are experiencing gossip going around in your work environment, simply approach the group that is perpetrating it. You can suggest to the group or other person, "Let's find a way to solve the issue you guys are talking about rather than gossiping about it." This kind of direct, solution-based thinking allows you to prevent further gossip and to create a meaningful pathway for them to follow. This also can inspire people to alter their behaviors about gossiping.

Think Before You Act

If you hear gossip going on about you, it is very important that you don't panic. People can become upset and react quickly. Instead of reacting immediately, take your time and see if you can control your feelings so you can keep from making the spiral bigger. Often our interpretation of what people say has more impact on us than what was actually said. So, take your time and ask yourself, "What really happened?" Separate the facts from the story.

Make a Request

If you hear gossip coming from a group, one of the most powerful countermoves is to make a request that people do not talk behind each other's back. Assert that they should not talk negatively about each other. You can also request that they take the issue to the person directly.

***

None of the above strategies are possible without having a high level of integrity yourself. If you really honor a pledge to yourself that you will not gossip, you will be able to alter this behavior.

With such a pledge, you also have the power to hold others who are gossiping accountable for their actions. Most people don't realize that they have the power to do that, but you can do it if you commit to acting with integrity in all conversations.

Here is a suggested list of things you can say when you hear people gossiping:

- "I'd like to request that since we are all equal, we speak positively about each other. If there is anything that is bothering any of us about another person, talk to the person directly and not with others. Will you accept my request?"
- "I need to be frank with you. I do not like hearing people talk about other people behind their backs. How would you feel if people were talking about you behind your back?"
- "I appreciate all of you. This is a workplace of professionals and we should do everything to keep it that way."
- "We are here to work as a team. Gossip can break

up our team and is unhealthy. What do you say we stay as a powerful team and don't talk behind others' backs?"
- "It makes me uncomfortable talking about other people while they are not here. I request if you have something negative to say, either say it directly to the person and don't get others involved, or just let it go,"
- "I am committed to having a strong working relationship with you, and I am committed to getting along with you. Gossiping breaks up relationships and I don't want that to happen. What do we need to do to have a strong relationship? Would you be willing to give up gossiping?"

The workplace bottom line is this: You either need to find the courage to directly confront the person or contact someone in your company who can do something about it. Or, you simply must have the courage to let it go. However, if you do choose to let it go, you will have encouraged the gossiper to continue gossiping knowing nothing will be done about it.

Also keep this in mind: If you choose to let it go, you cannot let it come up again.

Perhaps the best thing you can do is give them this book as a gift.

Appendix A
THE EVOLUTION OF GOSSIP: THE REST OF THE STORY

The word "gossip" is derived from the Old English word, "godsibb." This translates to "from god and sib" and generally points to the term for the good parents of one's child or the parents of one's godchild.

In the sixteenth century, the word assumed the meaning of a person, most often a woman, who delights in idle talk. Other common words for this personality were a "newsmonger" or a "tattler."

In the nineteenth century, the term's definition was extended. It went from being used to describe the speaker to the conversation between two such persons.

The term also denotes conversations originating from the bedroom at the time of childbirth. When a woman was about to give birth, the process used to be a social event with a wide reach, exclusively attended to by women. The pregnant woman's female relatives and neighbors would gather to sit with her and chat.

Over time, gossip came more to mean talk about other

people. Some suggest that gossip comes from the same root as "gospel." It is a contraction of "good spiel," meaning a good story.

For gossip to evolve at all, however, we first needed the basic forms of language. According to Melissa Hongeboom, a UK science journalist, language came out of our common ancestors, the apes, and appeared somewhere between six and thirteen million years ago.

Apes tend to spend most of their day grooming each other. They touch and stroke each other's fur and bodies, often picking out bugs, debris or dirt. Our earliest human ancestors are likely to have also groomed each other as well.

Robin Dunbar of the University of Oxford in the UK believes these initial grooming behaviors served a hygienic purpose. However, in the course of primate evolution, these behaviors also came to serve a social purpose. This amazing theory, supported by evidence, says that this grooming is a way for apes to show their loyalty and fidelity to one another.

Monkeys and apes only build relationships with a limited number of associates. Their grooming ritual is a one-to-one activity that takes time. This mechanism of bonding "imposes an upper limit on group size," says Dunbar. The mechanism may have been the evolution of gossip, communicating about one another and harnessing the newly appearing skill of language. Gossiping allows individuals to "groom" several people simultaneously.

We can only speculate about the complexity of the

language skills of our human ancestors, as no physical or fossilized evidence can survive to document the spoken word.

Gradually, as the Homo erectus lineage continued and produced our forebears, language came into being. One version of a gene vital for modern language evolved into its current form about 200,000 years ago.

***

Another popular idea about the origins of gossip, first proposed in the 1990s, is that humans rely on gossip to maintain our very valuable social bonds. In the early days of human beings, the main activity was hunting and providing for the family. At night they lived in fear that some other creature in the wild might eat them. Once they discovered fire, they would gather around the fire at night and try to stay awake so they could survive.

When shared language came into existence, humans could have conversations. Through this communication, they could attribute meaning to events in their lives. As our early human ancestors moved out of the forest and into more open areas, there came a much greater need to work together to successfully hunt for food.

This required a higher degree of teamwork. People had to share personal information. "This social supportive aspect of human nature allowed gossip to come about", says Klaus Zuberbuehler, a school of psychology and neuroscience professor.

Religions have specific attitudes toward gossip.

THE EVOLUTION OF GOSSIP: THE REST OF THE STORY

According to Judaic teaching, gossip consists of words spoken without purpose. This is also known as evil tongue or "lashon hara" and is viewed as a sin. Speaking negatively about people, no matter how true it might be, counts as sinful behavior, because it demeans the dignity of others.

The Christian religion's perspective on gossip is typically based on a more modern view of the phenomenon. It is especially rooted in the assumption that generally speaking, gossip is negative speech. According to Proverbs 18:8, "The words of a gossip are like choice morsels. They go down to a man's innermost parts."

According to Apostle Paul's Epistle, the Romans associate gossips ("backbiters") with a list of sins including sexual immorality and murder. "Backbiters are haters of God, despiteful, proud, boasters, inventors of evil things and disobedient to parents."

According to Matthew 18, Jesus Christ also taught his followers that conflict resolution among members of his church ought to begin with the aggrieved party attempting to resolve their dispute with the offending party alone. Only if this path to resolution does not work would the process escalate to the next step involving another church member and then the public.

Phil Fox Rose, a New York editor and blogger at Patheos.com writes, "We must harden our heart towards the 'out' person. We draw a line between ourselves and them and define them as being outside the rules of Christian charity. We create a gap between ourselves and God's love." As we harden our heart toward more people and groups, Rose continues, "this negativity and feeling of separateness will grow and permeate our world, and we'll find it more difficult to access God's love in any aspect of our lives."

The Bible's New Testament also favors group accountability. Ephesians 5:11; 1st Tim 5:20; James 5:16; Gal 6:1-2; and 1 Cor 12:26 are all passages that may be associated with gossip. All of them are simply saying that talking negatively about others is sinful.

The Islamic tradition considers backbiting the equivalent of eating the flesh of one's dead brother. According to Muslims, gossiping harms its victims without offering them any chance of a defense.

This is akin to dead people who cannot defend against their flesh being eaten. Muslims are expected to treat others like brothers regardless of their beliefs, skin color, gender, or ethnic origin. This is derived from Islam's concept of brotherhood amongst its believers.

The Baha'i faith considers backbiting to be the "worst human quality and the most great sin." By this logic, even cold-blooded murder would be considered a less reprehensible activity than backbiting.

Baha'utulla stated, "Backbiting quenches the light of the heart, and extinguishes the life of the soul." When someone kills another, it affects the physical being. However, when someone gossips, it affects one more profoundly.

Robin Ian MacDonald, a British anthropologist and

evolutionary psychologist, claims gossip originated as a way of helping bond disparate groups of people that were constantly growing in size.

According to MacDonald, gossip became a social interaction that helped a group of people gain information about other people without personally speaking to them. He found that sixty-five percent of gossip conversations consist of social topics.

REFERENCES

"Gossip." Dictionary.com. Accessed November 6, 2019. https://www.dictionary.com/browse/gossip.

Harari, Yuval Noah. *Sapiens: a Brief History of Humankind*. New York: Harper Perennial, 2018.

Shapiro, Steve. *Listening for Success: How to Master the Most Important Skill of Network Marketing*. USA: Chica Publ., 1999.

Schwantes, Marcel. "9 Ways to Get Rid of Workplace Gossip Immediately." Inc.com. January 25, 2017. https://www.inc.com/marcel-schwantes/if-you-do-these-things-you-qualify-as-a-gossiper-which-research-says-can-ruin-yo.html.

Miller, Joshua. "12 ways to deal with coworkers who gossip" https://www.linkedin.com/pulse/12-ways-deal-coworkers-who-gossip-joshua-miller/.

www.ingramcontent.com/pod-product-compliance
Lightning Source LLC
LaVergne TN
LVHW011726060526
838200LV00051B/3038